PIANO · VOCAL · GUITAR

CONTEMPORARY THEATRE BALLADS

CONTENTS

ISBN 0-634-06798-2

HAL•LEONARD®
CORPORATION
7777 W. BLUEMOUND RD. P.O. BOX 13819 MILWAUKEE, WI 53213

Visit Hal Leonard Online at
www.halleonard.com

BREEZE OFF THE RIVER

from THE FULL MONTY

Words and Music by
DAVID YAZBEK

A CHANGE IN ME

from Walt Disney's BEAUTY AND THE BEAST: THE BROADWAY MUSICAL

Words by TIM RICE
Music by ALAN MENKEN

To Coda

I still de - pend u - pon
For now I re - a - lize

had dis - ap - peared for good.

that good can come from bad

That may not make me wise _____

_____ but oh it makes me glad And I _____

I nev - er thought I'd leave be - hind _____

ELABORATE LIVES
from Walt Disney Theatrical Productions' AIDA

Music by ELTON JOHN
Lyrics by TIM RICE

I'm so tired __ of all __ we're go-ing through   I __ don't want to

live like that __   I'm so tired   of   all we're go-ing through __

I don't want to   love like that   I just want to be   with you __

Now and for - ev-er, __   peace - ful,

HOW DID WE COME TO THIS?

from THE WILD PARTY

Words and Music by
ANDREW LIPPA

OUR KIND OF LOVE
from THE BEAUTIFUL GAME

Music by ANDREW LLOYD WEBBER
Lyrics by BEN ELTON

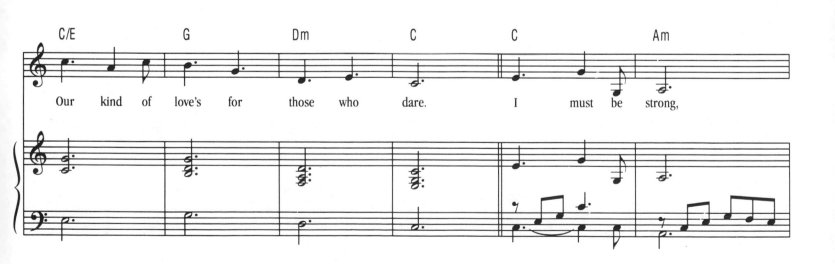

I shall____ cling to him with____ all my might.____

It's   my   right.____

I KNOW WHERE I'VE BEEN

from HAIRSPRAY

Music by MARC SHAIMAN
Lyrics by MARC SHAIMAN and SCOTT WITTMAN

Gospel Ballad tempo

MOTORMOUTH

There's a light_____ in the dark-ness,_____ though the

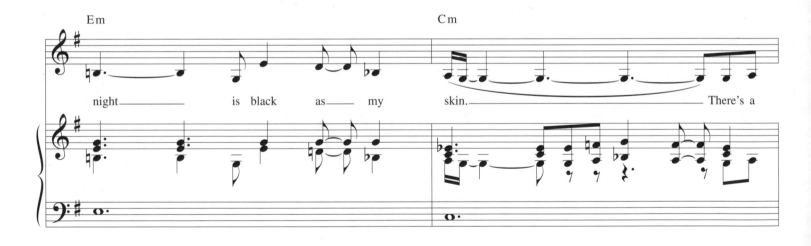

night_____ is black as_____ my skin._____ There's a

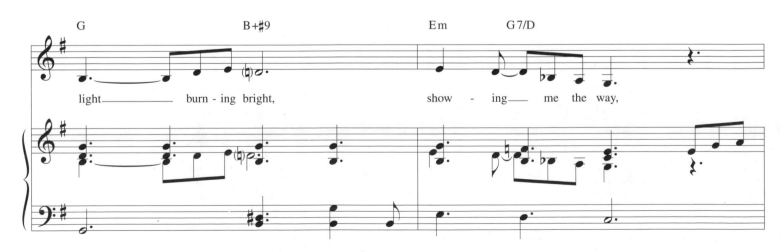

light_____ burn-ing bright, show-ing_____ me the way,

I TURNED THE CORNER

from THOROUGHLY MODERN MILLIE

Music by JEANINE TESORI
Lyrics by DICK SCANLAN

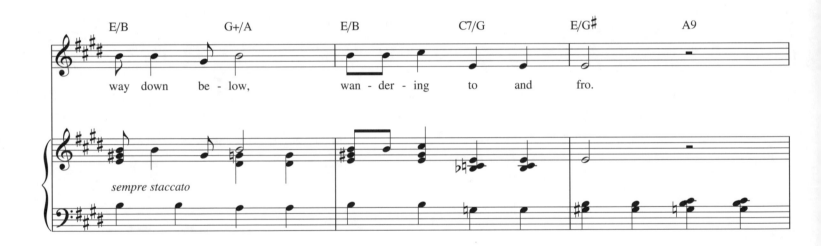

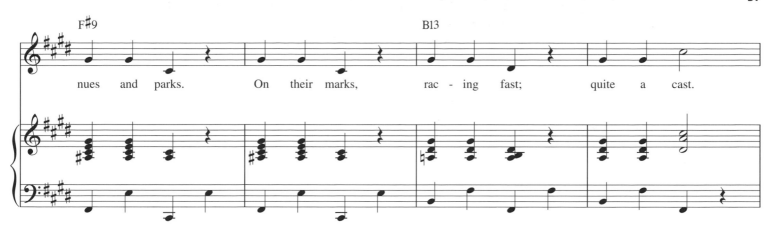

nues and parks. On their marks, rac - ing fast; quite a cast.

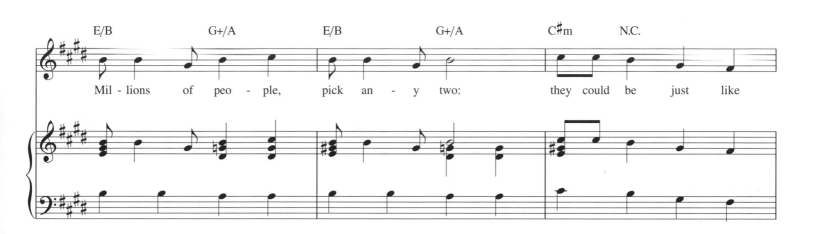

Mil - lions of peo - ple, pick an - y two: they could be just like

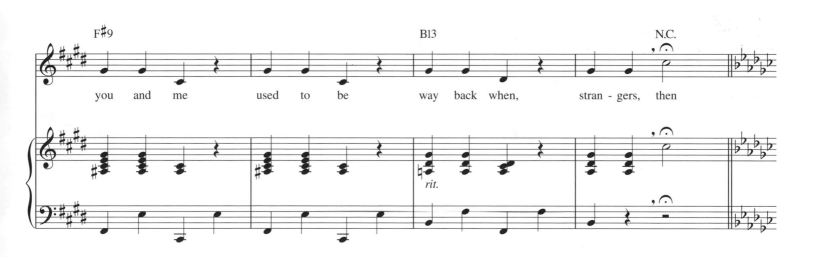

you and me used to be way back when, stran - gers, then

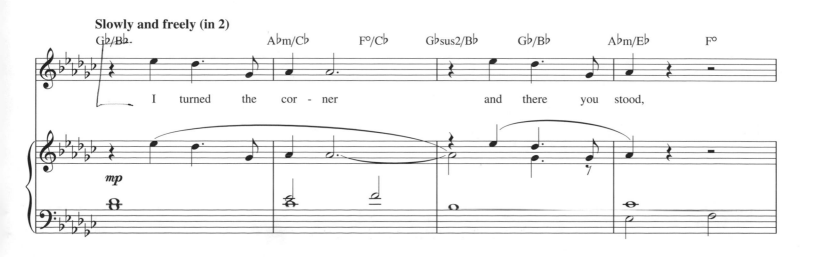

I turned the cor - ner and there you stood,

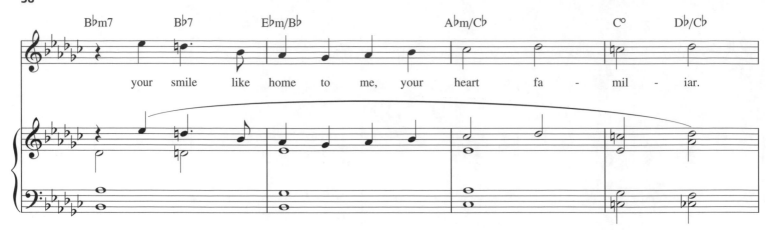

your smile like home to me, your heart fa - mil - iar.

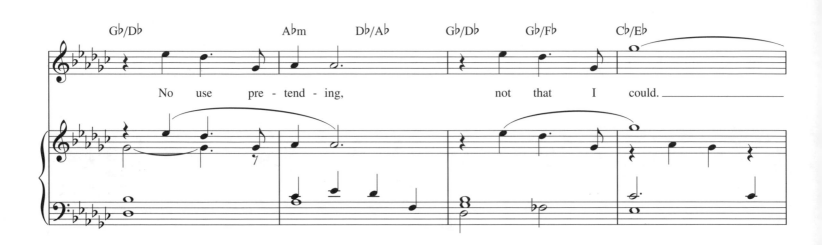

No use pre - tend - ing, not that I could. _____

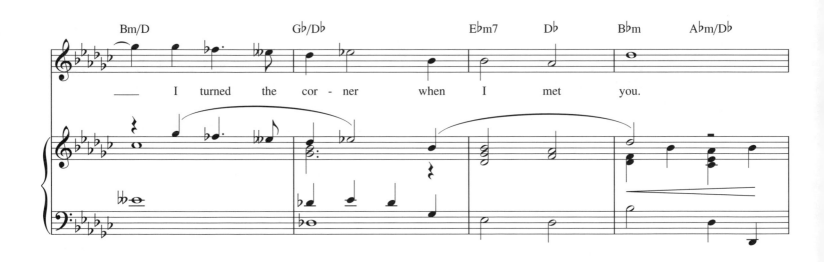

_____ I turned the cor - ner when I met you.

Moderately slow (in 2)

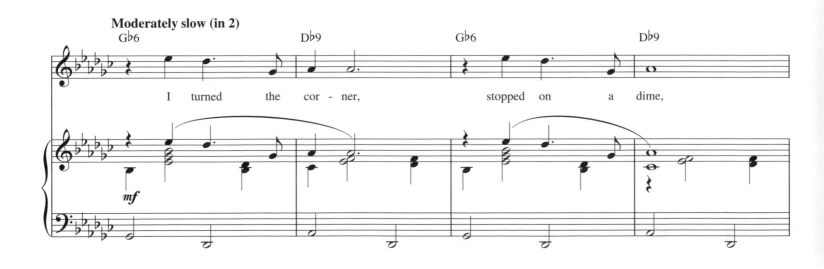

I turned the cor - ner, stopped on a dime,

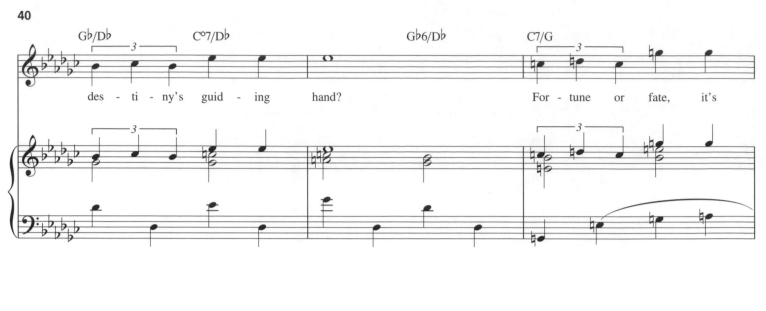

des - ti - ny's guid - ing hand? For - tune or fate, it's

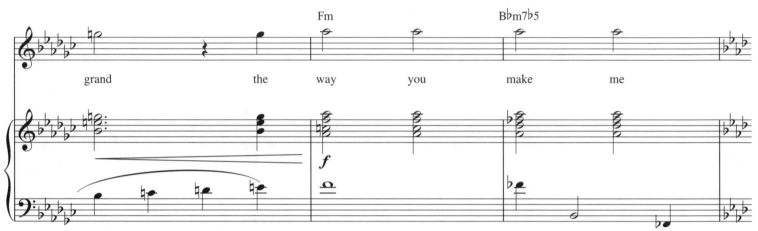

grand the way you make me

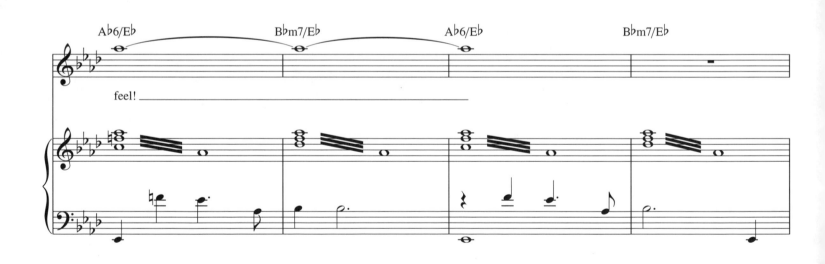

feel! _____

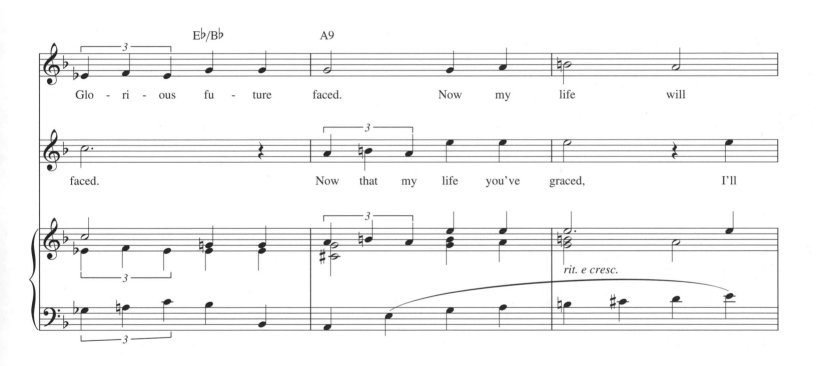

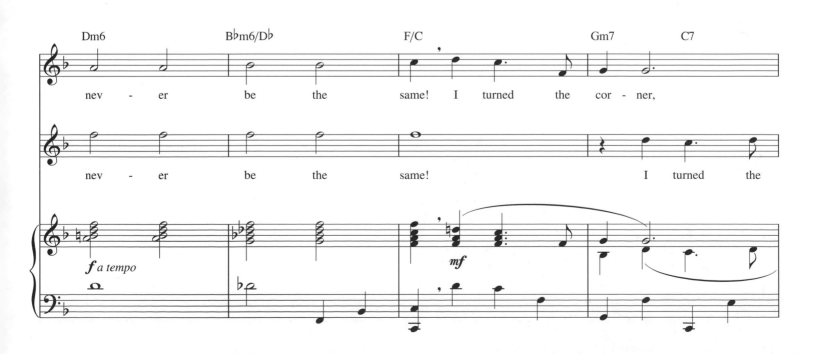

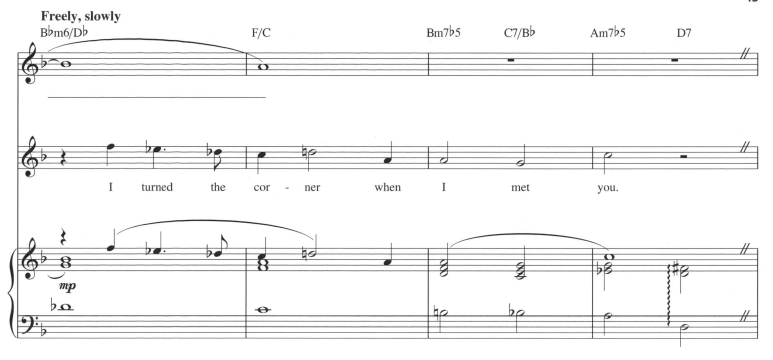

Freely, slowly

I turned the cor - ner when I met you.

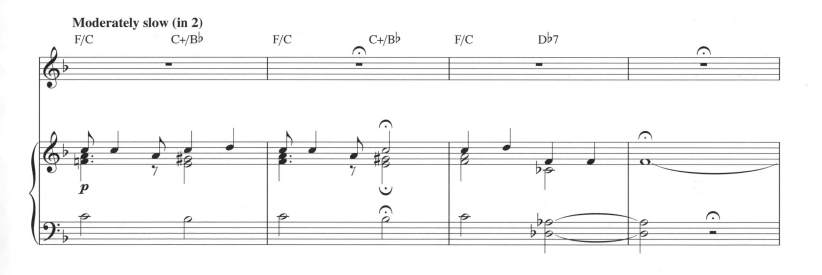

Moderately slow (in 2)

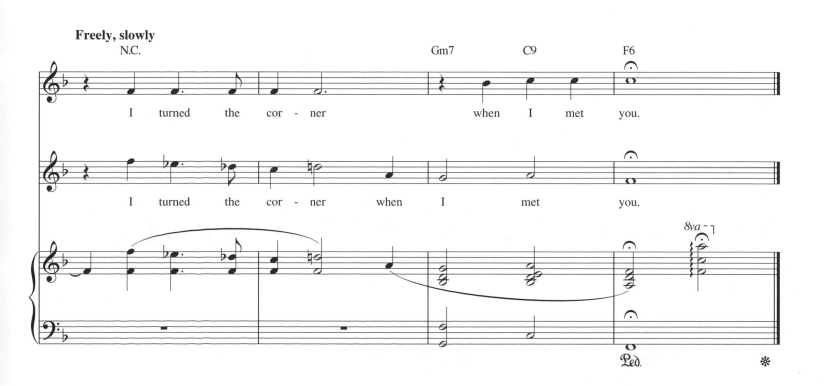

Freely, slowly

I turned the cor - ner when I met you.

I turned the cor - ner when I met you.

IF I CAN'T LOVE HER

from Walt Disney's BEAUTY AND THE BEAST: THE BROADWAY MUSICAL

Music by ALAN MENKEN
Lyrics by TIM RICE

no com-fort, no es-cape. _____ I see, but deep with-in is

With more motion

ut - ter blind - ness. Hope - less, _____ as my

dream dies. _____ As the time flies, _____ love a

rall.

a tempo

lost il - lu - sion. Help - less, _____ un - for -

LAUGHING MATTERS

from Howard Crabtree's WHEN PIGS FLY

Music by DICK GALLAGHER
Lyrics by MARK WALDROP

Jay: Live At Five and C N N keep us all a-breast of

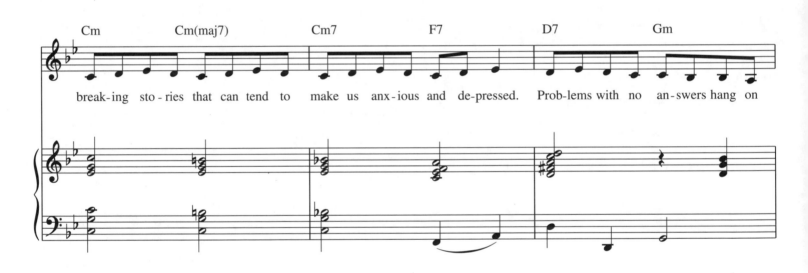

break-ing sto-ries that can tend to make us anx-ious and de-pressed. Prob-lems with no an-swers hang on

like some nag-ging cough, and ev-'ry day some brand new "is-sue" rears its head to piss you off.

THE NEXT TEN MINUTES
from THE LAST FIVE YEARS

Music and Lyrics by
JASON ROBERT BROWN

Flowing (♩. = 64 - 66)

JAMIE

Will you

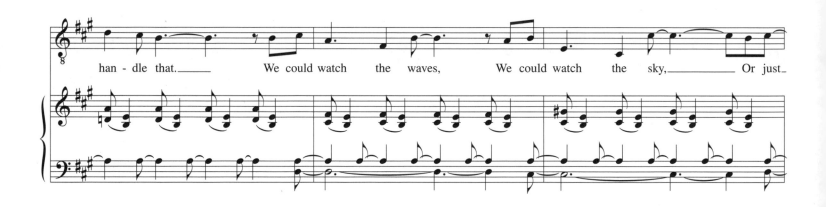

share your life with me For the next ten min-utes? For the next ten min-utes: We can

[*Ped.* throughout, change pedal on new harmonies]

han - dle that.___ We could watch the waves, We could watch the sky,___ Or just___

___ sit___ and wait___ As the time ticks by,___ And if we make it 'til___ then,___ Can I

ask you a - gain___ For an - oth - er ten?___ And___ if

you in turn a - gree To the next ten min - utes, And the next ten min - utes,___ 'til the

mor - ning. comes, Then just hold - ing you___ Might com - pel me to___ Ask___ you for

more._____ There are so man - y lives I want to share

with you;___ I will ne - ver be___ com - plete un - til I

CATHY

I am not

do.___

al - ways on time. Please don't ex - pect that from me. I will be

late, But if you can just wait, I will make it e - ven - tu - al - ly. Not like it's

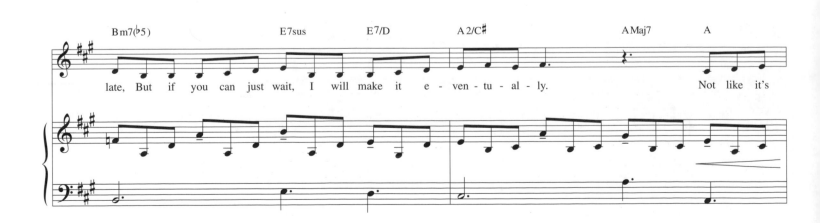

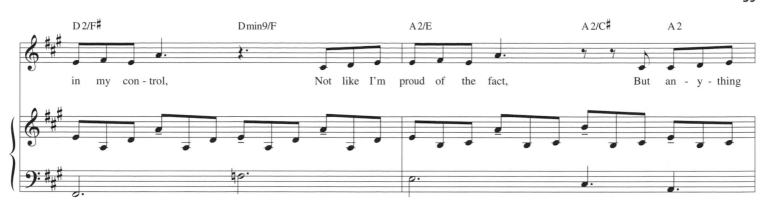

in my con-trol, Not like I'm proud of the fact, But an-y-thing

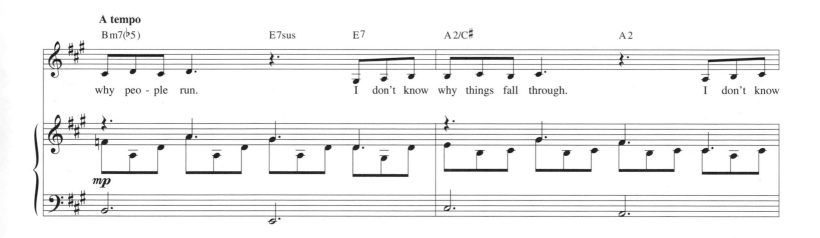

oth-er than be-ing ex-act-ly on time I____ can do.____ I don't know

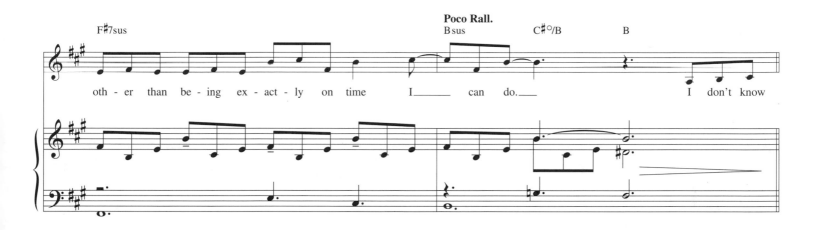

why peo-ple run. I don't know why things fall through. I don't know

how an-y-bo-dy sur-vives in this life With-out some-one like you. I could pro-

ONE MORE BEAUTIFUL SONG

from A CLASS ACT

Words and Music by
EDWARD KLEBAN

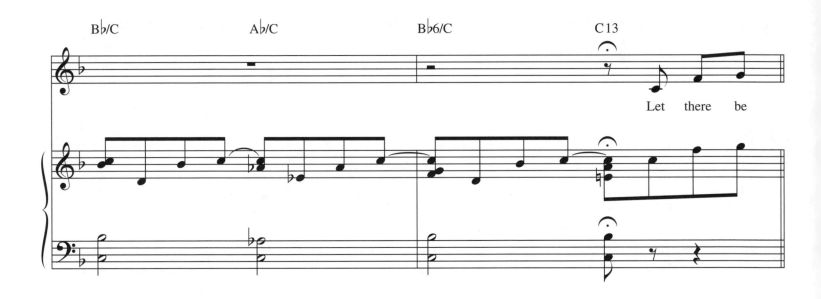

Let there be

one more beau - ti - ful song in the cos - mos, Let there be

SHADOWLAND

Disney Presents THE LION KING: THE BROADWAY MUSICAL

Music by LEBO M and HANS ZIMMER
Lyrics by MARK MANCINA and LEBO M

Chorus:

And where the jour- ney ____ may lead you, __ let this prayer ____ be your guide. Though it may take you __ so far-a-way, ____ al- ways re- mem- ber your

SOMEONE LIKE YOU

from JEKYLL & HYDE

Words by LESLIE BRICUSSE
Music by FRANK WILDHORN

I peered through win-dows, watched life go by. Dreamed of to-mor-row,
It's like you took my dreams, made each one real. You reached in-side of me

but stayed in - side. The past was hold - ing me,
and made me feel. And now I see a world

STARS AND THE MOON

from SONGS FOR A NEW WORLD

Music and Lyrics by
JASON ROBERT BROWN

Folk Rock, gentle (♩=60)

mp legato

I met a man with-out a dol-lar to his name,— who— had no traits of an-y val - ue but his smile

strength that will help you grow____ I'll give you

truth and a fu - ture that's twen - ty times bet - ter than an - y____ Hol -

- ly - wood plot." And I thought, "You know,____

I'd rath - er have____ a yacht."____

I met a man who lived his life out on the road,___ who___ left a wife and kids in Port - land on a whim.

I met a man whose___ fire and pas - sion al - ways showed,___ who___ asked if

STILL HURTING
from THE LAST FIVE YEARS

Music and Lyrics by
JASON ROBERT BROWN

Once the foun - da - tion's cracked And

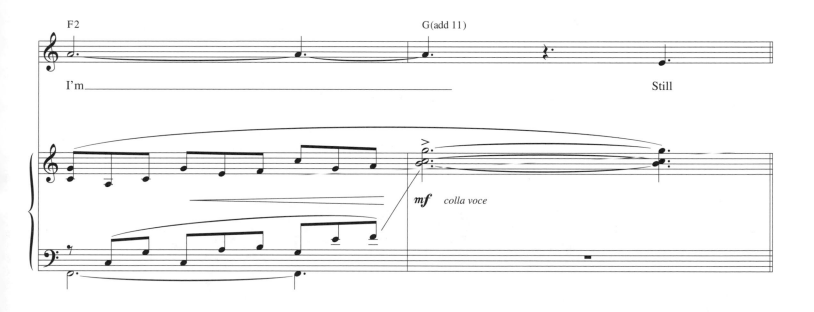

I'm___ Still

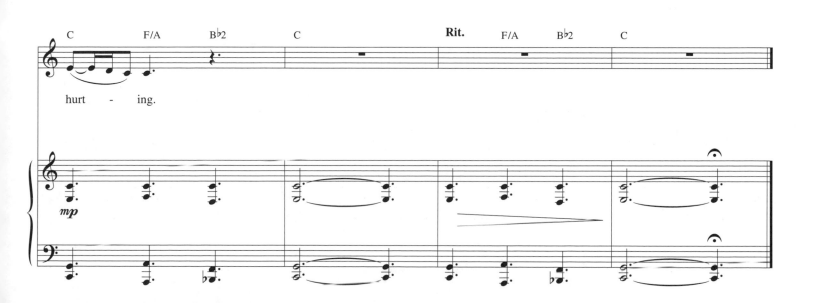

hurt - ing.

THAT FACE
from THE PRODUCERS

Music and Lyrics by
MEL BROOKS

THEY LIVE IN YOU

from Disney Presents THE LION KING: THE BROADWAY MUSICAL

Music and Lyrics by MARK MANCINA,
JAY RIFKIN and LEBO M

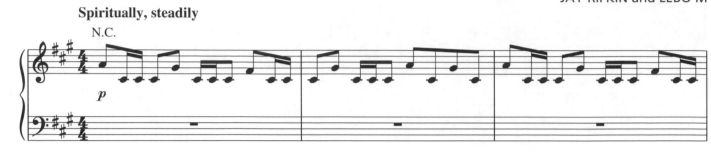

'TIL HIM
from THE PRODUCERS

Music and Lyrics by
MEL BROOKS

TIMELESS TO ME
from HAIRSPRAY

Music by MARC SHAIMAN
Lyrics by MARC SHAIMAN and SCOTT WITTMAN

WILBUR: Styles keep a-chang-in'. The world's re-ar-rang-in', but Ed-na, you're time-less to me. _____

126

WHISTLE DOWN THE WIND

from WHISTLE DOWN THE WIND

Music by ANDREW LLOYD WEBBER
Lyrics by JIM STEINMAN

WHO WILL LOVE ME AS I AM?

from SIDE SHOW

Words by BILL RUSSELL
Music by HENRY KRIEGER

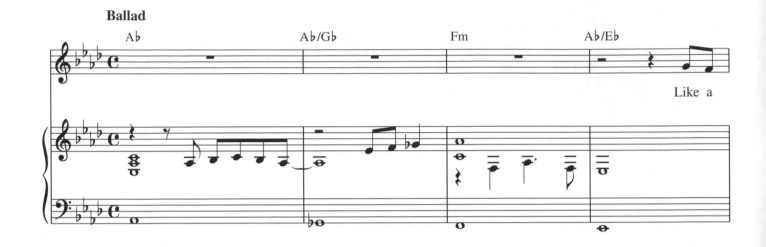

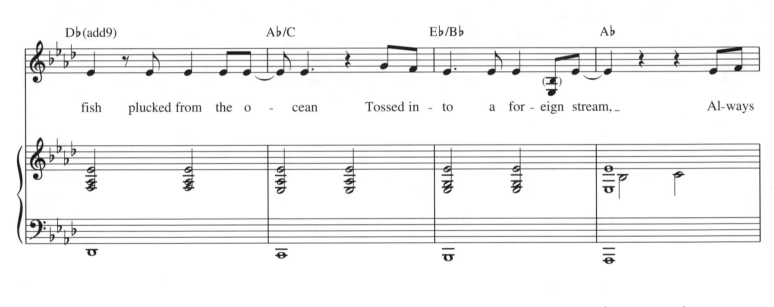

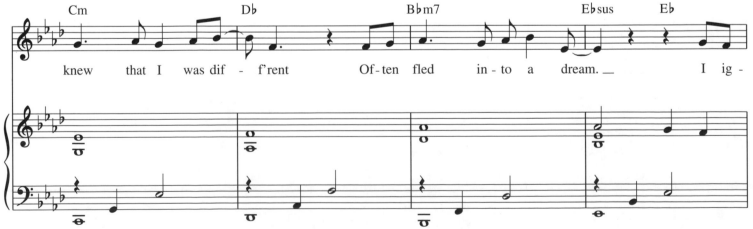

Daisy and Violet sing this number as a duet in the show; adapted as a solo for this edition.

*optional duet part

WITHOUT YOU

from RENT

Words and Music by
JONATHAN LARSON

YOU RULE MY WORLD

from THE FULL MONTY

Words and Music by
DAVID YAZBEK

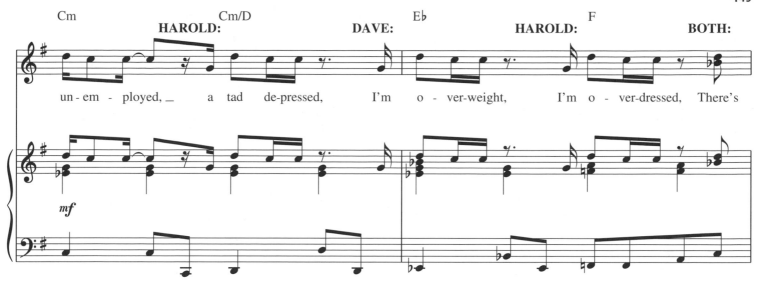

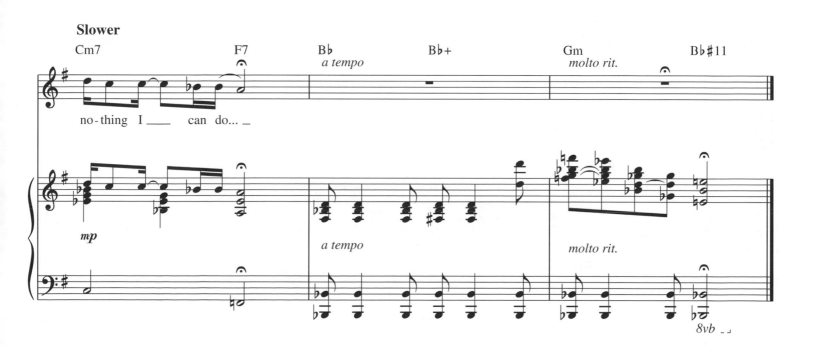

8vb

WRITTEN IN THE STARS

from Walt Disney Theatrical Productions' AIDA

Music by ELTON JOHN
Lyrics by TIM RICE

RADAMES:

You are all I'll ev-er want _ but this I am de-nied_

Some-times in my dark-est thoughts _ I wish I'd nev-er learned _

RADAMES:

AIDA: What it is to be in love _ and have _ that love _____ re-turned

AIDA: Is it

writ-ten in the stars? _ Are we pay-ing for some crime? _____ Is (that)

sub. p

YOU WALK WITH ME

from THE FULL MONTY

Words and Music by
DAVID YAZBEK

Moderately slow, but moving ahead

Is it the wind ___

o - ver my shoul - der? ___ Is it the wind that I hear gent - ly whis - per - ing

"Are you a - lone ___ there in the val - ley?" ___

Sing the top line melody in this section for a solo version of the song.

WE WROTE THE BOOKS ON BROADWAY

Hal Leonard is your source for the best selection of Broadway Music Books.

THE ULTIMATE BROADWAY FAKE BOOK - 4TH EDITION

Over 500 pages offering over 700 songs from more than 200 Broadway shows! Includes hits from *Jekyll & Hyde, Martin Guerre, Rent, Smokey Joe's Cafe, Sunset Boulevard*, and *Victor/Victoria*, and more! This is the definitive collection of Broadway music, featuring a song title index, a show title index, a composer & lyricist index, and a show trivia index. Songs include: Ain't Misbehavin' • All I Ask of You • As If We Never Said Goodbye • As Long As He Needs Me • Bewitched • Cabaret • Camelot • Castle on a Cloud • Day By Day • Do-Re-Mi • Don't Cry for Me Argentina • Edelweiss • Everything's Coming Up Roses • Getting to Know You • Hello, Dolly! • I Dreamed a Dream • If I Were a Rich Man • The Impossible Dream • Last Night of the World • Love Changes Everything • The Music of the Night • Oklahoma • On My Own • Only You • People • Seasons of Love • Send in the Clowns • Someone • The Sound of Music • Starlight Express • Tell Me on a Sunday • Unexpected Song • Waiting for the Light to Shine • What I Did for Love • and more!
00240046 Melody/Lyrics/Chords...$45.00

LOVE SONGS FROM BROADWAY

Includes 47 romantic favorites: As Long As He Needs Me • Can You Feel the Love Toonight • I Have Dreamed • If He Walked into My Life • If I Loved You • Just in Tiime • My Heart Stood Still • Someone Like You • Take Me As I Am • Think of Me • This Can't Be Love • more.
00310386 ....$14.95

THE BROADWAY BELTER'S SONGBOOK

A great new collection for women singers. All songs have been chosen especially for this type of voice, with careful attention to range and keys. 30 songs, including: Broadway Baby • The Lady Is a Tramp • Everything's Coming Up Roses • I'd Give My Life for You • Cabaret • Memory • and more. 176 pages.
00311608 ....$16.95

THE BEST BROADWAY SONGS EVER

We've made this book even better with the addition of songs from some of Broadway's latest blockbusters such as *Miss Saigon, The Phantom of the Opera, Aspects of Love, Les Miserables*, and more – over 70 songs in all! Highlights include: All I Ask of You • As Long As He Needs Me • Bess, You Is My Woman • Bewitched • Camelot • Climb Ev'ry Mountain • Comedy Tonight • Don't Cry for Me Argentina • Everything's Coming Up Roses • Getting to Know You • I Could Have Danced All Night • I Dreamed a Dream • If I Were a Rich Man • The Last Night of the World • Love Changes Everything • Oklahoma • Ol' Man River • People • Try to Remember • and many, many more!
00309155 ....$20.95

100 YEARS OF BROADWAY
100 Years In Times Square

In 1893, when 42nd Street in New York City was still considered "rural," the American Theatre was erected and the Broadway tradition began. The theatres have moved and been renamed, the musical styles have changed and evolved, and few shows from 1893 are remembered, but Broadway has thrived and flourished. This book brings together 100 years of memories with over 80 songs from shows ranging from *Babes in Toyland* to *Kiss of the Spider Woman*. It also includes synopses and photos from the shows. Songs include: Bewitched • Bonjour Amour • Comedy Tonight • Give My Regards to Broadway • I've Grown Accustomed to Her Face • The Impossible Dream • Love Changes Everything • Memory • Sun and Moon • You're the Top • and more.
00311642 ....$25.95

THE BIG BOOK OF BROADWAY – 2ND EDITION

Songs from over 50 shows, including *Annie Get Your Gun, Carousel, Company, Guys and Dolls, Les Miserables, South Pacific, Sunset Boulevard*, and more. 76 classics, including: All I Ask of You • Bali Ha'i • Bring Him Home • Camelot • Don't Cry for Me Argentina • Hello, Young Lovers • I Dreamed a Dream • The Impossible Dream • Mame • Memory • Oklahoma • One • People • Tomorrow • Unusual Way • and more.
00311658 ....$19.95

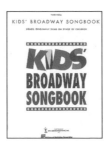

KIDS' BROADWAY SONGBOOK

An unprecedented collection of songs originally performed by children on the Broadway stage. A terrific and much-needed publication for the thousands of children studying voice. Includes 16 songs for boys and girls, including: Gary, Indiana (The Music Man) • Castle on a Cloud (Les Miserables) • Where Is Love? (Oliver!) • Tomorrow (Annie) • and more.
00311609 ....$12.95

Prices, contents, and availability subject to change without notice.
Some products may not be available outside the U.S.A.

FOR MORE INFORMATION, SEE YOUR LOCAL MUSIC DEALER, OR WRITE TO:

HAL•LEONARD® CORPORATION

7777 W. BLUEMOUND RD. P.O. BOX 13819 MILWAUKEE, WI 53213

www.halleonard.com

0202